Etching on a penny 1940

DUNDEE ART GALLERIES AND MUSEUMS
M^cMANUS GALLERIES

11th July – 22nd August 1987

ABERDEEN ART GALLERY AND MUSEUM

5th – 26th September 1987

WALKER ART GALLERY, LIVERPOOL
NATIONAL MUSEUMS AND GALLERIES ON MERSEYSIDE

6th October – 15th November 1987

First published 1987
by The Fine Art Society PLC
148 New Bond Street, London W1Y 0JT

Design & production by Ashted Dastor Associates
Printed in Great Britain by Paul Green Printing Limited.

ISBN 0 905062 01 9

JAMES

by

ROGER BILLCLIFFE

Published by

THE FINE ART SOCIETY

148 NEW BOND STREET LONDON W1Y 0JT TELEPHONE: 01-629 5116

for

CITY OF DUNDEE DISTRICT COUNCIL

Frontcover shows Plate 29 **The Tay Bridge from my Studio Window**

PREFACE

The Fine Art Society is proud to have prepared this book celebrating McIntosh Patrick's 80th birthday year. He first exhibited at our London Gallery about 1930 and, apart from the 60th birthday exhibition presented by Dundee Art Gallery in 1967, the few one-man shows he has had have been with us.

Roger Billcliffe, who directs The Fine Art Society's Scottish Galleries has produced a perceptive and finely-written account of the artist's long career and has set this very Scottish artist in his appropriate context in the wider world of art.

The exhibition for which this book/catalogue has been produced includes almost every important work painted by the artist and Clara Young, Keeper of Art at Dundee Art Gallery, deserves the greatest praise for her steadfast and sympathetic dedication to the task of mounting this definitive tribute.

ACKNOWLEDGEMENTS

It has long been the intention of Dundee District Council to organise a major retrospective exhibition as a tribute to James McIntosh Patrick on the occasion of his 80th birthday. This exhibition has had one forerunner: in 1967 we put on a splendid large show of McIntosh Patrick's works which was very successful and drew large crowds. However, it lacked a lasting memento in the form of an illustrated catalogue. Now this is amply rectified, thanks to the generous initiative of The Fine Art Society, which has prepared this superb illustrated biography which is, unbelievably, the first book on this artist to be published.

A great many people have been involved in a project of this size. First and foremost, I should like to thank all the private individuals and the staff of art galleries and other institutions who have so kindly agreed to lend their pictures for the exhibition. I am also grateful to the many other collectors who showed me their paintings and gave me their time and hospitality. It would have been easy to double the size of the exhibition!

We are greatly indebted to Ron Thompson and Grampian Television for making the lively and entertaining video of the artist at work which accompanies the exhibition. D. C. Thomson & Co Ltd. kindly assisted and allowed access to their files. I greatly appreciated the help received from my many District Council colleagues. I am immensely grateful to Roger Billcliffe and Andrew Patrick for their invaluable help and advice: they were co-selectors of the exhibition as well as being the makers of this book. I think I should have been lost without them. Finally, my special thanks are due to McIntosh Patrick himself for his unfailing charm, cheerful patience and enthusiastic encouragement – and also just for being his delightful self.

This exhibition has been made possible by generous financial assistance from the Scottish Arts Council and sponsorship from the following bodies, to whom we owe a great debt of thanks:-

The General Accident Fire & Life Assurance Corporation PLC
Macfarlane Group (Clansman) PLC
Tullis Russell & Co Ltd.
Veeder-Root Ltd.
Smith Hood & Co. Ltd.

Clara Young Keeper of Art
City of Dundee District Council Art Galleries and Museums

INTRODUCTION
by Lord Provost Thomas Mitchell, J.P.

McINTOSH PATRICK AND DUNDEE

JAMES McINTOSH PATRICK, the man and the artist, really needs no introduction to a local audience: his name is a household word in these parts. His works are immediately recognisable, while his vision of the Angus landscape is shared by two whole generations. We hope that Scots from all over the country will come and see this major retrospective exhibition which we have organised in his honour. Probably the finest landscape painter living in Scotland today, McIntosh Patrick has a special relationship with the town of his birth.

Demand for his original paintings outruns supply. There is normally a waiting list of about forty people, most of them Dundonians, all hoping for the chance to purchase his next painting. Often farmers and lairds while tramping their fields come across McIntosh Patrick immortalising their bit of land – and buy the work straight off the easel. Auction prices for the rare painting by him which come on the market are frequently higher than the price of a new picture.

Luckily for most, McIntosh Patrick paintings are widely available in the form of colour reproductions. Immensely popular with the Dundee public, several thousand of these prints adorn sitting rooms and living rooms throughout the City. His fame does not stop here: Scots abroad ensure that his works are spread the world over. A few years ago one of his prints was the best selling reproduction (by a foreign artist) in America: and every second ex-patriate Dundonian probably has a print of his famous "Tay Bridge from My Studio Window", an enduring image of one of the City's landmarks.

McIntosh Patrick is a "People's Artist". His personal popularity with the people of this city is phenomenal. He is frequently featured in the local press, often appears on television and his vivacity, sparkling humour and gifts as a natural and enthusiastic speaker ensure that he is constantly asked to give illustrated talks to various groups – Women's Guilds, Rural Institutes, Round Table, Probus, Rotary and many others. Once he gave the prestigious George Armitstead Memorial Lecture. All this culminated in 1979 when he was nominated "Dundee's Citizen of the Year", one of the most popular awards ever, in recognition of his services to art in Dundee and throughout the country. "I thought that that honour usually went to someone who worked in charity," he remarked on receiving the nomination. "But I am glad that someone thought that there are other ways to give people pleasure without giving them soup".

In recent years McIntosh Patrick has become directly involved in local good causes, often painting a picture at the request of a charitable group and allowing colour reproductions of it to be sold for the benefit of the organisation concerned. The print of his old school, Morgan Academy was extremely successful, the proceeds being of direct benefit to the school funds. Other fund-raising prints have included "Castle Hill, Dundee", 1983, for the St. Paul's Cathedral Fabric Appeal Fund (over £2,000 raised to date); "Beach Crescent, Broughty Ferry", 1985, for the Friends of the Orchar Gallery; and most recently a picture of the Magdalen Green Bandstand for the "Save the Bandstand Appeal".

Many members of the Royal Family own pictures by McIntosh Patrick, two of these being kindly lent for this exhibition. The large oil of Glamis Castle was a wedding present from the People of Angus to HRH The Princess Margaret; while the watercolour of the frigate Unicorn was a wedding present to TRH The Prince and Princess of Wales from the citizens and business community of Dundee, HRH Prince Charles having unveiled the new figurehead of the Unicorn in 1979.

The University of Dundee commissioned McIntosh Patrick to paint several portraits of distinguished academics and also the splendid large oil of Balgavies Loch. In 1973 they conferred on him the honorary degree of Doctor of Law. Dr Patrick has even closer ties with Dundee College of Art, having taught part-time at the School of Painting from 1930 to 1940. During the fifties and sixties his animated lectures on the history of art are remembered with great enthusiasm by his students. His famous open air sketching class has run every summer from the 1940s until today, while his well-attended Saturday morning class for adults is still going strong. In October 1986 Duncan of Jordanstone College of Art recognised over half a century of achievement as a painter and etcher by awarding Dr Patrick the Honorary Fellowship of the College. He is the first and as yet only artist to receive this honour.

McIntosh Patrick has endeared himself to the citizens of Dundee, both by his art and by his active participation in the life of the city. We are all very proud of his achievements. I would like to close by quoting the last paragraph of William Blain's introduction to the large McIntosh Patrick exhibition which we organised in 1967:

"The architectural and engineering influences of his early days have given him an understanding of how mountains hold themselves together, the purpose of trees in the landscape, how fields are formed. Under his fields are a network of drains; they are fields in which farm folks work. His houses have rafters and beams behind the stones and slates; they are lived in. His furrows have been ploughed and sown upon. In time the scenes he has commented upon will have passed away. James McIntosh Patrick's pictures will be teaching men to look at what is past, as they once taught men to look at what was present. Objective though personal, documentary though poetical, his works will still have appreciation and purpose and effect. Honesty in the application of high skill, will then, as now, as always, be seen to be the best policy".

Frontispiece **Keithick Mill** 1923 Oil 14 × 18 The Artist's Family

During the nineteenth century the popular image of Scotland was created by the painters of the vast panoramic landscapes which filled the walls of the Academies and Institutes of London, Edinburgh and Glasgow. They conformed with, and encouraged, the romantic notions of the Highlands evoked in a populace brought up on the novels of Sir Walter Scott and his imitators, where Rob Roy found a covert welcome in every glen, the noble stag was master of all he surveyed, and the climate veered uncontrollably between storms of hail and snow and livid sunsets reflected in the surface of disquieting lochs. It was a landscape unpeopled by human beings. Man had no effect on it. Farms and cottages, when they appeared at all in these huge set pieces, were shown derelict and broken down, deserted by their builders who had finally admitted to their defeat by the elements and had fled to more douce regions. That hypothetical visitor from outer space could be readily forgiven if, through knowledge of these paintings alone, he assumed that Scotland was entirely populated by sheep, woolly cattle and antlered beasts who stood proud against the snow, rain and fiery sun of this mountainous land.

A hundred years later and another, radically different view of the Scottish countryside captured the public imagination. In a time when even the wildest places of the Highlands have become much more accessible some of their mystery has inevitably disappeared. For many painters of this century there has been more attraction in the apparently commonplace. They have expressed more interest in a landscape which has offered man an opportunity to co-exist, a countryside which has not spurned his husbandry but which has openly responded to his care and his exploitation of its contour. This artistic change in direction has found ready support, for it chronicles the countryside that surrounds many of our major towns and cities. It is familiar to us, it is how we expect the countryside to look, but to examine it through the paintings of an artist like James McIntosh Patrick is to look at it with fresh eyes. Without realising it we are seeing the countryside as one man sees it and wants us to see it. We have been willing partners, however, and McIntosh Patrick, more than any other Scottish painter, and perhaps more than any other British painter of the twentieth century, has been popularly acclaimed throughout the world for his vision of a Scottish landscape which celebrates the role of man in its creation. His views of Angus and Perthshire have become icons of a modern landscape, which both in itself and in his paintings, has become accessible to us all.

I can't think of any period of my life when it wasn't taken for granted that I was always going to do something connected with drawing and painting. My father and brothers were architects and I had thought of following them but my mother was against that. Two architects in the family were enough for any household, she said, and so I suppose I thought I would become an art teacher.

JAMES McINTOSH PATRICK was born in Dundee on February 4th 1907. His father was Andrew Patrick, who worked with another Dundee architect, Charles Soutar. Soutar was a cultivated man who decorated his office with watercolours by James Watterston Herald (an Arbroath painter who worked very much in the loose style of Arthur Melville). Charles Rennie Mackintosh was one of Soutar's idols and he is believed to have owned a number of pieces of furniture designed by Mackintosh. From a very early age, James displayed a facility for drawing and painting that was the equal of his talented brother and father, himself a keen watercolour painter. By his 'teens his skills had overtaken theirs so that he was often to be found in his father's office drawing and colouring-in perspectives of the firm's latest projects. He began to paint in oils while at Morgan Academy and when he was 14 even started to experiment with etching, a medium in which he became quite proficient, more or less self-taught, before he went to art school. His family's natural assumption that he would follow a career in art culminated in a journey he made with his father to Glasgow in 1924 to enroll at the School of Art in Renfrew Street.

At that time, Dundee College of Art offered only a Diploma in Design and not in Painting, and McIntosh Patrick was drawn to Glasgow as much by his knowledge of the work of the Glasgow School of Painters as by the reputation of the Glasgow School of Art itself. In fact, Patrick can now wryly admit to confusing the painters with the institution but he was not the first nor the last to assume that they were one and the same. Certainly, many of the values held dear by Guthrie, Lavery, Henry and the other artists whom he admired, were still to be found in the teaching at the Glasgow School of Art so his expectations were not altogether unfounded. The quality of the work that he took along to his interview was such that the assessors allowed him to enroll for a three-year course, foregoing the customary first year where pupils studied all the different branches of art and design offered by the School. Although it was a considerable achievement to move straight into the second year, he now admits to missing the general grounding in calligraphy, design and other arts that formed the first year course.

By one of those strange coincidences that he says have marked his career, another young man was also admitted to the School on the same day on the same terms. Later that day Patrick discovered that this young man had taken a room in the same digs that Patrick and his father had chosen. The young man was Edward Baird who came from Montrose and although he and Patrick had never met before they became firm friends. Both painters were offered a post-Diploma Scholarship Year after completing their three years of study and both returned to the east coast in 1928. They kept in close

Fig. 1 **Near Ghent** 1922 Watercolour 13 × 9½ The Artist's Family

contact and Baird was Patrick's best man at his wedding in 1933 to Janet Watterston, whose father was a cousin of the painter Watterston Herald.

Baird and Patrick were consistent prizewinners in their year and their natural ability was recognised and rewarded. In his second year Patrick became monitor of the etching class and was given a studio of his own to work in. Etching was the field in which he had a head start over most of his contemporaries but he acknowledges the benefit of the teaching of Josephine Haswell Miller. Her husband, A. E. Haswell Miller (who was later to become Keeper of the Scottish National Portrait Gallery), encouraged his work in watercolour and provided a foil to any over-confidence he might exhibit:

I remember doing a series of watercolours for a friend in Dundee which were all in the style of Herald or Melville, all very blotchy and impressionistlc. Haswell Miller saw them and said they were OK, very clever and what have you, but they weren't really very good. "Look here," he said to me, "if the art of watercolour painting could be divided into twenty-four parts, then you have learned the first four and the last four, but the stuff in between is still very important. The next time you are in London go and look at the work of Henry Rushbury, that will show you what can be done with watercolour.

This was advice to which Patrick paid careful attention and the looser manner of Herald and Melville disappeared to be replaced by a tighter, more linear handling of the kind that Rushbury, Muirhead Bone and several of their contemporaries had adopted.

The Head of Drawing and Painting was Maurice Greiffenhagen, a painter who insisted on the maintenance of traditional values, particularly in composition. He was a man whom many students found distant, unbending and unsympathetic. Mary Armour, who was at the School just a few years before Patrick, remembers failing to win First Prize in her year, which all her contemporaries had expected her to take, because Greiffenhagen disapproved of her Diploma composition, which was a 'modern life' subject instead of a historical or religious theme as Greiffenhagen preferred. Patrick came to know him better almost by accident. In 1926 both Patrick and Greiffenhagen had spent three months of the summer vacation in Provence (the younger man's visit being financed by his earnings from working in the Glasgow docks during the General Strike of 1926) but they had not met each other there. On his return to Glasgow Greiffenhagen began a painting of the Pool of Bethesda but became stuck when he discovered that he had no drawings which were suitable for the background. Someone told him that Patrick had also been working around Carcassonne and Greiffenhagen asked to see his sketches. The background landscape was eventually completed from two of Patrick's drawings and master and pupil were drawn together through the shared experience.

The main product of this summer in France, however, was a group of etchings of Provençal hill towns such as Carcassonne and Les Baux. Patrick acknowledges the strong influence in these of the French etcher Meryon but the true source is to be found in Quattrocento Italian painting, particularly the work of Piero della Francesca and Mantegna, whose *Agony in the Garden* was a favourite painting of the young Patrick. Mantegna's perspective, the reality of the third dimension that he created through the fine detail in the background of his paintings had a profound effect on these early etchings. Patrick's family background in architecture almost certainly accounts for the accuracy of the detailing of the townscape in these prints but the fascination with the structure of the landscape is a pointer to the way his work would develop over the next decade.

In 1927 Patrick showed his etchings to a Dundee printseller

Fig. 2 **The Egotist** 1927 Oil 39 × 63 The Artist's Family

who, recognising their quality, decided to send them to his contacts in London. This was a period when great reputations and considerable fortunes were being made in the etching market. The Scots seemed to have a strong foothold in it, with the work of D. Y. Cameron, James McBey, Muirhead Bone, William Strang, W. D. MacLeod and others commanding keen interest in a highly competitive world. Many large collections were made; subscriptions were taken for the latest edition of an artist's work which was eagerly awaited; and proofs often changed hands several times, at ever-increasing prices, as soon as they were published. Colnaghi's, one of the leading London print dealers of the day, expressed a strong interest in Patrick's etchings and asked to be shown his next ten plates as they were produced, with the intention of preparing them for publication. Harold Dickins, another print publisher, took a different approach and asked the young man to go and see him in London.

Although he felt that the etchings he had seen could be improved, he decided to publish two of them – "as he said, I had to live and eat" – and he offered Patrick a contract of £50 a quarter for first refusal of his next few plates. He was happy with what was sent down to him over the next few months and by the time Patrick left the School of Art in 1928 he had an assured income of £200 per annum (with which he was able to repay the Maintenance Scholarship he had won in 1927), a car and a growing reputation as the 'coming man' in contemporary print circles. He also left the School with a clutch of prizes for portraiture and landscape painting and added to them the James McBey prize for etching, awarded by the Scottish Print Club. His friend Baird won the School's coveted Newbery Medal and the pair of them must have been in Sir George Clausen's mind in his Assessor's Report in 1927:

The School has at present two or three students of quite remarkable promise whose compositions would give distinction to any school.

Patrick's own Diploma Composition of 1927, *The Egotist* (fig. 2), drew heavily on his interest in architecture and his experiences in Provence. A fantasy of architectural styles in both existing and imaginary buildings, Patrick's awareness of the work of Bellini and Mantegna is clear in his handling of the perspective and the relationship between the figures and the landscape.

Harold Dickins published several of the French etchings, such as *Les Ramparts, Les Baux* (fig. 3), *Evening, Nîmes* (fig. 4) and *Palais des Papes, Avignon,* (fig. 5) in 1927 and 1928 and followed these with a series of Scottish landscapes – *Loch Lomond, Glencoe, The Pass of Glencoe* (fig. 6), *Wade's Bridge, Garve* and others – over the next two years. The French subjects are populated with the rather stylised figures which appeared in *The Egotist* but figures hardly ever appear in the Scottish subjects. These latter prints are very much concerned with the structure of the landscape, the grandeur of nature, but in most of them there is also to be found a growing pre-occupation with man's effect on his environment. At Les Baux Patrick was fascinated by the way the walls of the town had been built along the contours of rocky precipices and how the houses behind perched on the plateaux formed behind the ramparts. He took a high viewpoint and a high horizon with the valley falling away below the walls of the town and rising to the hills in the background. This format was changed slightly in the Scottish subjects, particularly in the Glencoe etchings where the mountains climb up above the level of the viewer as the old road through the glen snakes its way up the hill before us. Writing about Patrick's work in *Print Collector's Quarterly* in 1930, Max Judge highlighted an element of 'strangeness' in these etchings. He considered that Patrick was attempting to come to terms with the modern painter's rejection of the traditional representation of reality by redefining the importance of perspective in his work. Patrick's concept of pictorial space, he believed was conditioned by his

Fig. 3 **Les Ramparts, Les Baux** 1927 Etching 7 × 10 The Artist's Family

Fig. 4 **Evening, Nîmes** 1927 Etching 6 × 7½ The Artist's Family

Fig. 5 **Palais des Papes, Avignon** 1928 Etching 5 × 8½
The Artist's Family

Fig. 6 **The Pass of Glencoe from the Valley** 1928 Etching 6 × 8
The Artist's Family

anxiety to escape from the orthodox picture plane by using perspective as a recession instead of a projection; in this way perspective is given the new function of taking the eye through the picture to lose itself in it. Instead of attempting to bring all depth on to one plane, the painter's own eye has become like the lens of a microscope that is without any depth of focus, so that each plane must be observed in turn. Pictorial design becomes multi-planar and free from illusion.

The etchings were worked up from pencil sketches, similar to those made around Glasgow while Patrick was still at the School of Art (fig. 7 – fig. 13). These drawings, however, are much more factual, having none of the deliberate perspective that is introduced into the etchings. The element of strangeness that Judge noticed is in part due to the artist's use of these drawings as aides-mémoires, rather than as blueprints for the etchings. His memory of the scene played as much a part in the development of the etching as the drawings, the design being reworked until it conformed both to the image in the artist's memory and to his concept of 'rightness' in the design. The strong sense of pattern and design in composition that I find one of the most satisfying parts of Patrick's work, he dismisses as being automatic. He says that he has no pre-determined sense of pattern that he wishes to incorporate into his pictures but that he works at them until they are 'right'. This may be semantics, but it is typical of his approach to his art. Not accepting that a painter might suffer from an artistic equivalent of 'writer's block' he has always painted every day and has worked on the canvas, paper or plate until he arrives at an acceptable effect.

Drawings and watercolours also formed the basis for the artist's works in oil at this time and it is interesting to speculate on the different processes whereby a single series of drawings could produce such different results as the etching of Les Baux and the oil of the same subject. There is a greater

14

Fig. 7 **Wellington Church from Park Circus, Glasgow** 1925
Pencil & watercolour 6 × 7½ The Artist's Family

Fig. 8 **Trinity College, Glasgow** 1925 Pencil 9 × 6 The Artist's Family

Fig. 9 **The Forth and Clyde Canal, Port Dundas, Glasgow** 1925
Pencil & watercolour 8 × 6½ The Artist's Family

Fig. 10 **The Portico, Glasgow Art Gallery** 1925
Pencil & watercolour 7½ × 6½ The Artist's Family

Fig. 11 **The Forth and Clyde Canal, Dawsholm, Glasgow** ·1925 Pencil & watercolour 5 × 7
The Artist's Family

Fig. 12 **Farm at Balmuildy, near Glasgow** 1925 Pencil & watercolour 7 × 8 The Artist's Family

Fig. 13 **Avignon** 1926 Pencil & ink & watercolour 7 × 9½ The Artist's Family

freedom of handling in the oil painting and the detail which appeared in *The Egotist* has been suppressed in favour of a broader, more posterly handling. The eeriness of the etchings, the exaggerated sense of place, is not quite so apparent in the French oils as in those of Scotland, such as *Ardmair Bay* (1928) and *Ben Slioch, Loch Maree* (1929). The Mantegnesque perspective, however, is still apparent in these pictures; indeed, the landscape has more the feeling of a background to a figurative subject than a painting in its own right.

Although *Les Baux* (1927, pl. 2) was shown at the Royal Academy in 1928 and *Ardmair Bay* in 1929, etching remained Patrick's prime concern at this time. Frank Rutter and P. G. Konody, two of the leading critics of the day, praised his oils as they appeared at the Academy but Patrick was more impressed by the approval of F. L. Griggs for his etchings. Griggs' etched work, with its interpretation of the landscapes of Samuel Palmer, affected Patrick just as it did the young Graham Sutherland. Following Griggs' example, he composed his plates in strong contrasts of light and dark, inking them solidly to create a bold pattern of black and white which leads the eye firmly into the distance. Griggs became a staunch supporter of the young Patrick, proposing his membership of the Royal Society of Painter-Etchers, to which he was elected an Associate in 1932, and probably being instrumental in the decision of the British Museum Print Room to purchase several of his prints. His etchings were included in a number of the foreign exhibitions of British Graphic Art (organised by the forerunner of the British Council, the Department of Overseas Trade), as a result of which he was asked to show in several of the International Print Exhibitions in America, such as Chicago and Pittsburgh. As a final accolade, in 1935 he was invited by the Print Collectors' Club to execute a plate, *Kyleakin*, for presentation to its members.

By this time, however, the boom in the etching market had evaporated. As early as 1930 Dickins had decided not to publish any more editions of etchings, although he honoured his contract with Patrick and continued to pay a retainer. Patrick was forced to turn to other work to provide an income and he was appointed as a part-time member of staff at Dundee College of Art in 1930. Apart from his natural skills as painter and etcher, he was valued for his recent contact with the Diploma Course at Glasgow as the College in Dundee had by this time been authorised to offer a Painting Diploma of its own. But his immediate source of funds was through his contacts with the local press and he obtained a commission for a series of drawings of local landmarks which were published in the *Dundee Courier* throughout 1929 and 1930. The skills he had learned in his father's office, rendering architectural perspectives, repaid themselves and kept him provided with a steady income. Valentine's, the Dundee publisher of postcards and reproductions, commissioned a series of similar views, not just limited to Dundee buildings but covering towns all over Britain. These were produced from photographs and were retailed throughout the country in Woolworth's stores, under the trade name "Etchographs", until well into the next decade.

Having spent so long on his etchings since leaving Glasgow, his painting had been rather neglected but he was to return to it now, almost full time. He took out the drawings made on his visit to France and Italy in 1926 and began to paint in oils using these earlier sketches and etchings as a base. *Assisi* (1930, fig. 14) was one of the first of these paintings and it shows how Patrick was experimenting with an amalgam of his etching and painting styles. In 1931 he showed *The Church of St Francis, Assisi* at the Royal Academy, which was the first large scale painting he had made for three or four years. Although its handling was much tighter than that of the relatively loose 1920s landscapes, there was little of the crisp detail of the etching which had inspired it. The composition had a high foreground viewpoint with the hilltown and its

Fig. 14 **Assisi** 1930 Oil 12 × 16 The Artist's Family

Fig. 15 **Briggs' Men** 1936 Etching 7 × 10 The Artist's Family

basilica below the viewer and the surrounding fields stretching away into the distant hills. The light was strongly directional on the church and the wooded hills leading up to it but the distance was more evenly lit, merging into mists on the hills which gave the landscape a sense of eeriness that is often to be found in the etchings. The painting was hung on the line at the Academy, reproduced in the *Royal Academy Illustrated* and attracted considerable critical interest but it was unsold.

A similar treatment of landscape can be seen in one or two oil portraits which were contemporary with it but in these Patrick adopted a more detailed manner in the painting of the figures which gave the paintings the clarity of tone and line that are more readily associated with his etchings. Patrick had won prizes for his portraiture at Glasgow School of Art and one of his few surviving portraits of that period gives a pointer as to how his figurative work was to develop. *Dorothea Hannah* (1928, pl. 1) is a portrait with a strong sense of design in the rather deliberate pose of the sitter, who is silhouetted against a neutral background of draperies. The strong side-light emphasises the modelling of the features and helps to reinforce the sense of 'super-reality' that Patrick may have absorbed from Edward Baird's work of the period. The portrait of Alexander Russell (1930) is a more traditional composition, with the figure seated before a landscape background in the manner of a Renaissance portrait, a form which Gerald Brockhurst was returning to fashion. This landscape, evenly lit and contrasted with the directional lighting of the figure, again emphasises the slightly unreal quality of the subject.

Patrick's innate sense of design played a large part in the success of his figurative work of this period. It can be seen to emanate, as so much did at this time, from his etchings, although only one of these is a figurative composition, *Briggs' Men* (1936, fig. 15). Unusually for Patrick, this etching has a very tight composition with no view of the surrounding street in which the men are working. The rather abstract pattern which their kneeling forms create, silhouetted in dark ink against a pale background is one of his most assured compositions of the period. This dominant arrangement of light and dark is, in fact, a reversal of his most striking portrait, *The Rt Rev Monsignor Turner* (1932, pl. 3).

The commission to paint a portrait of Monsignor Turner came at a crucial time for Patrick. His work in oil was slow as he struggled with the new style that he was gradually formulating during 1932. *The Church of St Francis, Assisi* had not sold at the Royal Academy in London, despite its favourable reception, and his only income, apart from the seventeen shillings and sixpence he earned from his half-day at the Art College, was from the commercial work he was producing for the *Dundee Courier* and Valentine's. Given his fascination for – and his talents at manipulating – strong patterns of light and shade, a commission to paint a Roman Catholic prelate in his full robes must have seemed a God-send. The brilliance of the white surplice contrasted against the rich shades of purple and the luminosity of the sitter's head was silhouetted by the dark background to create a bold design. The pose of the priest, with the two strong diagonals of white-draped arms cutting across the purples, creates a lively composition and the delicacy and intricacy of the lace on the surplice allowed Patrick to display his technical virtuosity almost as never before. The picture was a success and had other events not overtaken his work as a portraitist, there is little doubt that he could have made himself a considerable reputation and a comfortable living from portraiture. Its reception gave both his financial and spiritual well-being a much needed boost, but above all it helped him rationalise the future direction his painting would take.

After the Assisi picture was returned from the Academy Patrick scraped it down and began to rework it. Eventually he put it aside and started work on another painting of Assisi, *The Cloth Market*, (begun 1931) but it remained unfinished and was destroyed in 1940. This was very different from the painting of the basilica, having numerous figures and a composition which was indebted to the artist's Diploma painting, *The Egotist*. The detail in the Turner portrait, however, suggested to the artist an alternative way forward and he began work in 1932 on a large landscape that was to radically change his style and way of working. Taking as a base the etching *The Pass of Glencoe* Patrick began work on a large oil which occupied him for the next two years. It has a limited range of colour which is due not only to the subject but also to its source in an etching. He admits to the picture, *The Three Sisters, Glencoe,* being an experiment, both in medium and technique and it reached its final appearance only after many months of detailed painting and reworking. The surface was rubbed down and areas polished and finely retouched to give it a subtle sheen of grey and silver that caused so much excitement when it was shown at The Fine Art Society in 1934. At one stage Patrick even washed the painting over with a solution of caustic soda and then glued the canvas down to a panel – "I wouldn't dare do that now". The painting of the swirling snows around the tops of the mountains is something with which he was very pleased, likening it to Chinese paintings. It is very much a tonal painting that, in its minute detail and its deliberate pattern of light and dark, is closely related to the etching of the same subject. The "strangeness" of the etchings was imported into the painting by the use of that deliberate perspective which he had first used in his graphic work. The road through the glen, along which a tinker family is making its way, is used to lead the viewer's eye into the composition. We are looking down on the road towards the bridge so that the foreground falls away sharply below us. As the road rises up to our level it also curves into the middle distance of the painting and provides the key to our understanding of its spatial organisation. It was a formula which the painter gradually honed over the next two or three years to create an effect which became a hallmark of his paintings. The viewer is made, by this device, to feel part of the landscape in front of him; Patrick creates an immediate relationship between the viewer and the inhabitants of his paintings suggesting a world shared between reality and illusion.

The painting was submitted to the Royal Academy in 1934 but it was rejected and Patrick contacted Harold Dickins to ask him to collect it and keep it in London.

I asked Dickins to keep it in London because I was terrified that if it came back to Dundee I would start to rework it. I had wiped out the Assisi picture and Glencoe had taken me the best part of two years and I couldn't face going through all that again. Anyway, Dickins kept it for a few months and then the new road through Glencoe was opened and it was in all the newspapers and Dickins suddenly realised that he had a topical picture on his hands. My picture was of the old road, when you set out in the morning and hoped to get to the top by the end of the day if the weather didn't change; and all of a sudden everybody wanted to know. Dickins took it along to The Fine Art Society in Bond Street and they were amazed by it and put it in the window. I didn't know any of this until I was reading a criticism of the Royal Society of British Artists by Frank Rutter in one of the Sunday newspapers. He didn't like the show but he finished off his review by saying something like "while there is nothing of special interest in this year's RBA there is in a window in Bond Street a painting which must be one of the great modern works of art". It was all very exaggerated, very grand stuff, very flattering for a young man to read. Then I had a letter from Griggs. "I knew you could etch", he said, "but I didn't know you could paint. I've just seen a picture in Bond Street that I want to buy for the Tate and the Chantrey Trustees will meet next week so I

will recommend that they see it before then." Anyway, somewhere along the line something went wrong and someone went into The Fine Art Society and bought it before the Trustees had their meeting. So, Griggs wrote to me again and said that the Trustees had liked it and that I was to send another picture for them to see at the Royal Academy next year.

Despite its failure at the Royal Academy, *The Three Sisters, Glencoe* was to change Patrick's fortunes and dictate a path that he was to follow until he joined the army in 1940. One immediate result was that The Fine Art Society said it would take any picture of his that Dickins cared to send. This arrangement continued up to the end of the war, with Patrick sending his work to Dickins who sold it through The Fine Art Society. In 1946 Dickins felt that his role had become superfluous and he stood aside, leaving Patrick and The Fine Art Society to form a direct relationship, and the firm remains his agent today. Patrick had married Janet Watterston in 1933 and he was thankful to have the support of a prestigious London Gallery during the difficult years of bringing up a young family.

Although the prospect of having a painting purchased for the Tate was a great incentive, Griggs had issued a deadline that did not allow him to spend two years on his next picture and he had only a few months before the sending-in day at the Academy. To compound his problems, Griggs then asked for two works for the exhibition and Patrick spent the weeks at the beginning of 1935 in feverish activity. He chose another winter scene for his main picture and painted *Winter in Angus* in the early months of the year. The subject owes more to his experience as an etcher than it does to the weather of 1935, as Patrick admits to being drawn, at this time, to the narrow tonal harmonies of black and white, light and dark, which were easier to re-create in oil in a snow scene. The sense of involvement with the landscape and the activity of the figures within it is much stronger here than in the Glencoe painting, partly because the human activity takes place much closer to the viewer and partly because the distant landscape is more of a backdrop than the real subject of the painting. The building in the foreground is Powrie Castle but its relationship with the surrounding landscape is all part of Patrick's imagination.

This is the first of the series of paintings which for many people have become the archetypal icons of the Scottish pastoral landscape, a landscape that has been cultivated by man for hundreds of years. While the farmer was adjusting and defining its contour for practical reasons he also created, almost by accident, a landscape that never seems threatening or unwelcoming and one which has an innate sense of pattern in its shapes of fields with their boundary hedges and graceful trees. 'Man-made, not God-made', is how McIntosh Patrick is said to like his nature and it is for this man-made landscape that he first began to invent new patterns of his own. That he was so successful at it is attested to by the number of people who are sure that they have seen and visited the sites of *Winter in Angus* and the other paintings which followed it over the next three or four years, not realising that they are the product of the painter's imagination.

His landscapes were synthesised from a series of drawings and watercolours made on the spot in the countryside around Dundee. A tracery of trees against the sky, a distinctive arrangement of farm buildings, the dry-stone dykes snaking their way around fields, a ploughing team making its combed pattern in the red soil were all to be noted down in the sketch-book he took out with him. Back in the studio in Ward Road, Dundee, with its neutral north light, the painter would assemble his sketches, isolating a favourite motif and combining it with a suitable partner until the composition seemed 'right'. This synthesis of individual landscape features enabled Patrick to improve on both man and nature in creating in the studio a landscape with an unerring sense of balance and design which strikes an immediate rapport with the viewer. Patrick now believes that the studio itself had a lot to do with his way of working. It had a high window, which gave a good light but no view, and this made the painter concentrate on his work without the distractions of the world around him. Not being able to compare his drawings with what he might see through the window made him rely more heavily on his visual memory. How the process worked for *Winter in Angus* is best described in the artist's own words:

The castle came because I had already made a painting and an etching of Powrie Castle and I thought it would make a good subject for a big picture. But in Winter in Angus *I created an imaginary viewpoint, up high. For the background – well I wanted a complicated background and at that time I was teaching on Fridays at Glenalmond and the background is the view from the Art Room window which I fitted in behind the Castle. I was looking for something for the foreground and I decided to put in the pigeon loft but apart from that the rest of the foreground is just invented. In those days – and I don't now know how I did it – I had a way of putting on paint and then rubbing something all over it to soften the image and then sharpening it all up by careful reworking. I let the paint make the suggestions into something more solid. In other words these were abstractions which gradually were turned into realist pictures. The concept was abstract but the means was realism.*

Winter in Angus was painted quickly by the standards of *Glencoe* but Patrick had very little time to produce a second painting for the Academy. He returned to the large Assisi picture, rubbed down and lying in a corner of the studio and reworked it in a similar manner, sharpening up the details and creating a crisp focus in the background landscape. When he sent this to the Academy in 1935 someone objected that it had been seen there before, which was not allowed by the Academy's rules. Fortunately, because it had been illustrated on its first appearance in 1931, Patrick was able to show that it had been almost entirely repainted and was now a very different picture from that submitted before. His explanation was accepted and both paintings were hung on the line in the Academy in 1935. Griggs was true to his word and *Winter in Angus* was bought by the Trustees of the Chantrey Bequest for the Tate Gallery. Compounding his success, *St Francis, Assisi* (pl. 4) was sold to the National Gallery of South Africa and a small portrait, *Marion*, (1935, pl. 7) won the Guthrie Award at the Royal Scottish Academy the same year.

Encouraged by this abrupt reversal in his fortunes, Patrick spent the summer of 1935 hard at work. He was still taking some subjects from his earlier etchings, such as *General Wade's Bridge* (1935) but two large paintings begun that year had no such antecedents. Harold Dickins suggested to him that he might follow the success of the winter picture by painting the other seasons and it was in Dickins' mind to issue the paintings as collotype reproductions. He put forward the subject of the first of them, *Springtime in Eskdale* (1935, pl. 13), as he had heard that it was the centenary of the engineer William Telford, who built the Caledonian Canal and many roads and bridges, and whose family lived in Eskdale. Patrick discovered the farmhouse where he was born and made it the subject of the painting. *Autumn, Kinnordy* (1936, pl. 10) was painted at the suggestion of The Hon. Mrs Lyell, who had admired *Winter in Angus*.

Both paintings follow the general formula devised for *Winter in Angus*. They have a high viewpoint, looking down sharply to the foreground and thus creating an exaggerated perspective with the features of the landscape laid out before us almost in plan form. The backgrounds are painted in the same sharp detail, creating a depth of focus which give the vistas an unusual clarity. It was a technique which he had developed for his etchings, but on the larger scale of these paintings it is seen at its most panoramic. Despite the apparent familiarity of the scenes, we know from the artist that they are again an amalgam of different parts of the country arranged to satisfy an abstract concept of design and pattern. This sense of pattern is clearly discernible in the arrangement of walls in *Springtime in Eskdale* and of fields and hedges in *Autumn, Kinnordy*. In each picture a lane is used to lead the eye deeper into the composition while human figures go about their business in the foreground. Despite the detailed and painstaking technique, the overall concept is an abstract one. The synthesis of real and imagined is a celebration of traditional painterly pursuits and is not concerned with the fidelity to the subject that is Patrick's main aim in his more recent paintings.

The pictures were hung at the Royal Academy in 1936, consolidating Patrick's reputation; the Walker Art Gallery, Liverpool, bought *Eskdale* and Mrs Lyell bought *Kinnordy*, which she presented to Dundee Art Gallery in 1948 in memory of her son, Antony Lord Lyell VC. In 1937, the last of the four seasons paintings, *Midsummer in East Fife* (1936, pl. 8), was also shown at the Academy, where it was purchased by Aberdeen Art Gallery. This was a different picture from the others, having an unusual composition with a knoll of old trees which cut the canvas in half. To the left the land falls away steeply, past grazing cattle and sheaves of corn in the fields to a distant view of the sea. On the right, in a clearing under the trees, a tinker family cook their midday meal over an open fire and the distant countryside is seen through a frame of foliage. There is a lyrical quality about this painting which owes more to a historical concept of landscape than do the other paintings. A landscape tradition stemming from Claude and Rubens is much more apparent here, while the other pictures of this date have something intrinsically modern about their compositions and handling. Influences on

Patrick in these paintings are easy to identify, and although he admits to knowing what was going on around him he feels that the similarity of atmosphere in much of his work and that of his contemporaries is due to "something in the air".

The particular direction of Patrick's stylistic development can be specifically attributed to his training in Glasgow. The influence of old masters such as Mantegna and Brueghel – the latter becoming more direct in the paintings of the seasons – remained conscious but they were gradually replaced by more contemporary painters. Although Patrick never met him, the influence of Frederick Cayley Robinson, who had taught in Glasgow earlier, was still very noticeable in much student work in Glasgow in the mid-1920s. It had had a distinct effect on James Cowie, whose work was well known in the city and both Patrick and the young Ian Fleming responded to it. Cowie eventually became the Warden of Hospitalfield House near Arbroath and he and Patrick came to know each other well in the late-1930s. He watched the painting of *Midsummer in East Fife* but his main influence is on Patrick's figurative work. One aspect of the young Patrick's stay in Glasgow which had a less obvious effect, but one which was very deep-rooted, was his contact with the work of Charles Rennie Mackintosh. Like many students at the School, Patrick responded in a positive way to the building itself. Mackintosh's interest in Scottish vernacular architecture and the way in which he combined such traditional motifs in the new Art School would certainly have been noted by a painter who himself had a keen eye for the details of the farm buildings of his native Angus. Mackintosh's strong sense of design, apparent in both his buildings and his paintings, was surely absorbed, however unconsciously, by the young and impressionable Patrick. He would not have seen Mackintosh's late watercolours, painted in France in the 1920s, but the visual approach of both artists has much in common.

In England a number of painters had adopted an approach similar to Patrick's. A pre-occupation with landscape, its physical forms, its uses and our relationship with it, was typical of many British painters in the 1930s. It was almost as if the painters had determined to record what would soon be lost to mechanisation or the impending threat of war. The lyricism and the romance of the countryside remained the province of the older painters, who had worked through or survived the fighting of the Great War, while the younger generation displayed its concern for landscape's material values, recording it with detachment for future generations. This surveying of the countryside, a concern for its industries, for its daily life, a fascination with the mix of natural and man-made shapes, can be seen in several pictures by Stanley Spencer and his brother Gilbert and in much of the work of Rowland Hilder, John Nash, James Bateman, Evelyn Dunbar and Douglas Percy Bliss. Eric Ravilious, with a more deliberate intent, began a series of paintings of rural industries but they are more concerned with the impact of mechanisation and the disturbance of the countryside by the non-agricultural industries than with the daily life of the professional farmer. These pictures have been described as surveys of rural England, and in his own way Patrick was doing the same for Scotland – although his interests were in nature itself and the activities of the farmer – selecting that which seemed important to him after studying the landscape at close quarters.

The paintings of the four seasons were followed by other rural subjects in a similar vein, exploring variations of the theme which he had now made so securely his own. *The Ettrick Shepherd* (1936, pl. 11) was shown at the Royal Academy in 1937 and bought by Manchester City Art Gallery. Unlike many of the other paintings of the 1930s this picture depicts an actual place – the farm leased by the poet James Hogg, author of *The Ettrick Shepherd*. Patrick had come across the farm on holiday in the summer of 1936 and had thought it a wonderful subject for another snow scene in the synthetic manner of *Winter in Angus* but on discovering that it was the actual farm which Hogg had worked he decided to create a more factual record of it. The picture follows the same general arrangement of *Winter in Angus*, with a high viewpoint, a focal point of interest in the arrangement of sheep-pens in front of the farm buildings and a distant backdrop of snow-covered hills. In the summer of 1937 Patrick spent several weeks with the Dickins family at Wellshead Farm on Exmoor. The sketches he made here are among his most detailed of farm buildings and the daily life of the farmer and his family. One incident he remembered was when the local hunt came through the yard and he was to make this the central event of a major painting, *An Exmoor Farm* (1938, pl. 12). From a quick sketch made on the spot, Patrick worked up the subject into his next exhibit at the Royal Academy in 1938, where it was bought by the Ferens Art Gallery, Hull. Despite the temptation to use a camera to provide the raw material for these large paintings, Patrick always remained true to his sketch book, preferring, even at this stage to select what he wanted to record, rather than be faced with the unwanted information that a photograph would include. The degree to which his synthesis of the landscape could be taken is illustrated here in that the original sketches are not of a snow scene – Patrick created the effect from his imagination. Furthermore, some thirty years later he had a letter from Sidney Gilliatt, the film producer, who wanted to identify the farm to use as a film location. Patrick told him where it was but Gilliatt wrote, after visiting Exmoor, to say that it was unsuitable after all. He had specifically wanted a farm which had a distant view of the sea and he was disappointed when he got to Wellshead to discover that the sea was not, in fact, visible from the farm as it was in the picture:

Apparently it was crucial for the purposes of the story that you should be able to see the sea from the farm and the painting had seemed so real to Gilliatt that he never thought that it was in part an invention. And then I remembered that the whole of the back part of that picture is done from another fairly detailed drawing from Dunkery Beacon and that behind the farm there was really not much more than a smooth green field that sloped up to the skyline with the river Exe running along at the bottom. And I just left off that hill and imagined what you would see if it wasn't there.

Winter had by now become a favourite subject and at the end of the 1930s Patrick painted several snow scenes. Although they all have quite different compositions, the general schema of a road or land leading one's eye into the vista had by now become his preferred format. Whether it be virtually obliterated by a heavy fall of snow, as in the snow-bound village in *Winter in Pethshire* (1938, pl. 14), a lane curving its way across the canvas, like that in *Sidlaw Road* (1936, bought by the Pittsburgh Art Gallery), or a steep hill leading vertically into the centre of the picture, such as the icy course created by the sledging children in *Sidlaw Village, Winter* (1936, pl. 9), Patrick used the device to create an immediate link between the viewer and the landscape. The latter painting shows the format to the greatest effect. The perspective draws us sharply down the hill, and our eye is led directly into the middle of the painting, encouraged by the speeding children, hurtling down into the village. The road and the horizon are linked by the tall trees with their filigree of branches on the right, with the distant snow-clad hills appearing between their branches.

The painting was bought by Frank Pick, the Vice-Chairman of London Transport, who was so impressed by Patrick's work that he asked him to design a number of posters for London Transport. *Happy Days of Cheer Again* (pl.17a), a poster for Harrow Weald station, is typical of the posters he made for Pick and the other railway companies who were later to employ him. A strong design had always been an important element of his paintings and he was well-equipped to translate the basics of his work in oil into a more graphic medium. That sense of unreality which was always present in his oils, no matter how detailed their execution, gave his posters an added dimension. As with his Scottish oils, people identified themselves with the subject and the poster's message was conveyed immediately. Following the successful reception of these first posters, Patrick was asked to produce designs for several of the main-line companies, usually but not always, with a Scottish theme. Patrick's posters of Edinburgh, Loch Lomond, the Border Abbeys, the Firths of Tay and Forth became known to millions of people throughout England and Scotland, ensuring that his image of the countryside became theirs. In the days when the companies used to decorate their carriages with views of the areas which they served, it was not uncommon to have Patrick's vision of the Angus countryside as company for several hours on a journey north from London.

By the end of the decade McIntosh Patrick's fortunes had reversed from the somewhat dismal outlook of 1930. Through hard work and with a helping of good fortune he had become one of the most successful young painters working in Scotland. His work was beginning to show some signs of change, notably an increase in topographical subjects. In the last years of the 1930s he exhibited a series of paintings of houses and castles, such as *Traquair House*, (1938, pl. 15), *Castle Campbell* (1938), *Spynie Palace* (1938), *Brodie Castle* (1939) and *Glamis Village* (1940, pl. 24). The degree of invention in these pictures was less than that in the paintings of the four seasons and Patrick was also involved in painting portraits (Professor Gordon Campbell in 1939 and Lord Lyell in 1940), which demanded a more literal approach. He had by this time, however, moved out of his studio in Ward Road, with its north light, and was working in his house in a studio which faced

south and which he found less conducive to his usual way of working. In 1939 he had moved with his wife and young family, Andrew and Ann, into a Georgian house on Magdalen Green overlooking the River Tay. "It was so close to the Tay Railway Bridge, which was reckoned to be a prime bombing target, that nobody wanted to buy it, but it seemed a perfect house for a painter and his family." It was a sign of Patrick's optimism that he should take such a bold step when the future seemed very uncertain but he was not altogether unconcerned about what lay ahead. It was in expectation of his being conscripted into the army that he began a painting of the garden of his new house showing his wife, Janet, hanging out the washing while his daughter played at her feet, *A City Garden* (1940, pl. 18)

This was a picture where his usual practice of assembling the composition from several drawings was abandoned and the result is a more or less factual account of the scene before him. This was a deliberate choice as, given the uncertainties facing both his country and his family, Patrick wished to record that particular moment of his life and the appearance of his garden before the commencement of his master plan for its development. He could not use his normal device of a lane or hedge to draw us into the picture but he chose a typical high viewpoint from a bedroom window and imposed a strong decorative and structural design on the composition. The diamond of the washing line with its white sheets and shirts cutting through the green of the lawn counters the linear pattern of the garden walls and the roofs of the factories in the background. Bright in colour, with a strong directional lighting, *A City Garden* is one of his most remarkable and accomplished paintings. It was shown at the Royal Academy in 1940 and bought by Dundee Art Gallery.

The expected call-up into the services came in 1940 and Patrick joined the army where he was trained as a tank driver before being commissioned into the Camouflage Corps. It was perhaps not unexpected, given his profession, but it was his knowledge of the countryside that was put to more use than his talents as a painter. The only time these received official recognition was when he took over the design and painting of the sets in the theatre at Catterick Camp while he was undergoing his basic training.

There were a lot of direct commissions of artists into the camouflage corps, several of whom were well known then or have since become quite famous. We all knew how artists like Wadsworth had been involved with painting the Dazzle ships during the First World War but what I had to do was totally different. My CO had written the classic text book on animal camouflage which showed how animals not only adapted their colours to harmonise with their background but also modified their behaviour so as not to draw attention to themselves, and that's basically what military camouflage is about.
I remember when I had just left Training School how we had to prepare for any retaliation for the Dieppe Raid which was being planned. We had to build bases for mobile anti-aircraft guns and it was my job to camouflage these bases, huge plugs of concrete in the fields. First I had to persuade the gunners to position their guns at the edges of the fields where there was natural cover from hedges and trees. Then I had to make sure that the contractors, with their huge lorries, used the fields in the same way that a farmer would. A farmer doesn't cross the middle of his fields, he sticks to the side so I had to make the drivers think like farmers. All their tracks, when seen from the air, looked like farm vehicle tracks, driving around the edge of the fields. That's a simple example but it shows how I was able to use my knowledge of what happened on a farm. Of course, it was all different in North Africa – there are no deserts in East Fife – but the principles were the same.
One of the first things I had to do was to change the colours

of the army vehicles which were coming out of North Africa. Not only did we have to repaint them for the Italian campaign but we had to rethink how we might confuse the German spotter planes. There's no way you can hide a tank in the desert no matter what colour or pattern you might paint on it but you might persuade the enemy that you only had twenty when you really had fifty and so on. We did this with nets and other bits of material which would eliminate shadows and confuse the photographs. All that had to change as the armies prepared to invade Italy.
It's silly, but one of the biggest problems I ever had was when I was in charge of the Camouflage Division at the School of Military Engineering in Capua. I used to drill the troops as to how they should black-up and decorate their helmets with twigs and dull down all the shiny bits on their webbing and rifles. Then they had to turn up for Guard Duty with blancoed belts and gaiters because their CSM refused to let his men go on duty "unless they were a credit to the Regiment." I was trying to stop them getting killed and he was more concerned with regimental pride and honour. It's a funny thing, the army mind.

Patrick did no official work as a War Artist and spent a lot of his time close to the Fronts in North Africa and Italy, latterly at Capua where he helped train other Camouflage Officers, including the late Sir William Coldstream. Painting, as he had practised it before the war, was out of the question but he did make time to sketch in pencil and watercolour whenever he could (pls. 20–24). He had always drawn out in the open air but the differences here was that these sketches were not intended as notes for paintings to be made in the studio. They reflect the strong light and colours of the Mediterranean countries, all of which was captured in watercolour. His use of this medium was out of necessity, as he had no space in his kit for oil paints and canvases, but he came to enjoy the speed with which he could work. Gradually, his handling of water-colour and gouache changed and he began to make pictures which he could regard as almost finished, as opposed to the brief notes and sketches he had previously made with water-colour. In 1946 The Fine Art Society exhibited these water-colours and drawings in London and the show then transferred to Aitken Dott in Edinburgh and Robertson and Bruce in Dundee, the first time that Patrick had had a one-man show in Scotland. It was well received and almost all of the pictures sold, which encouraged him to pay more attention to his work in the medium.

Four years of living outdoors, of having the sky, the sun and the wind for partners had a profound effect on his observation of the landscape. It certainly changed his relationship with it. No longer did he see the purely abstract elements of the countryside as being the most suitable material for his paintings but it took a little while for him to rationalise this with the style he had developed for his work in oils. When he returned to Scotland he took up more or less where he had left off, with paintings of buildings and pastoral scenes such as *Airlie Castle* (1946, pl. 26) and *Unthank Farm,* (1947, pl. 28) both of which were completed in the studio from sketches made out of doors. Just as the Ward Road studio had contributed to the formulation of his style in the 1930s, so his new studio in his house in Magdalen Yard Road brought about major changes in his work after the war. He no longer had the even north light which he had found so suitable, because his new studio faced south with a view of the Tay from which the sunlight glinted and reflected at a thousand angles. He found its glare distracting and totally at variance with the effect he was trying to create and so he began to take his easel outside to paint direct from nature as he had done in watercolour during his time in the army.

The first painting he finished in this way was *Glamis Village* (1946, pl. 25), a return to one of the subjects he had painted before he was called-up in 1940. Although the situation was different, painting *en plein air* rather than in the studio, his detailed handling remained the same. Despite the good results he achieved, he was disappointed in the length of time he wasted waiting for the same conditions of light and weather to re-occur. He decided, therefore, to forsake the studio-induced style of the 1930s in favour of painting direct from his subject and to adapt his handling to suit. As if to underline his new departure one of the first paintings produced after 1946 was to take advantage of the qualities of light in his new studio that he had previously avoided. *The Tay Bridge from my Studio Window* (1948, pl. 29) captured the glint of sunlight on the water as the afternoon sun cast long shadows across Magdalen Green. It may not have been painted out of doors but the picture reflects what Patrick could actually see from his window, rather than a compilation of what would have looked 'right'. Only the railings and gates come from his memory, the originals having been removed during the war, and they are inserted here to complete Patrick's record of how the house looked when he had moved in eight years earlier. The picture is, in fact, a companion to *A City Garden*, and the two paintings are intensely personal statements by the artist. They act as icons for particular phases of his life, the earlier painting made during the uncertain months at the beginning of the war and the later picture looking forward to a new phase of the painter's career. If *A City Garden* can be said to bring the work of the 1930s to an appropriate close, then *The Tay Bridge* opens the next chapter of his life.

In 1947 the Patrick family took a holiday on Easdale, an island in the Firth of Lorn, and Patrick produced a series of landscape paintings which are very different from those of his native Angus. *Easdale* was one of a series of paintings of the west coast of Scotland where, for the first time since the 1920s, Patrick was confronted with nature "in the raw", as he calls it. His response to it was not as sympathetic as it was to the cultivated hills of the east. Perhaps it acted as a catalyst, because he returned to Dundee with a definite concept of how he should proceed. In 1948 he saw in Glasgow the big touring exhibition of the work of Van Gogh and he was deeply impressed by the immediacy of Van Gogh's landscapes, particularly the way that it seemed as if he were standing in the same field or orchard as the artist. He felt that this was exactly what he wanted to achieve, and combined it with his new approach to naturalism to ensure that he captured the realism of the landscape in front of him. The panoramas of the 1930s paintings were no longer uppermost in his mind; what he wanted to do was to make the countryside and the weather in his paintings as real for the viewer as it had been for him.

From the end of the 1940s for the next three decades, Patrick produced the works for which he is now best known. Gone is the synthesis of individual features to make a satisfying composition; gone is the emphasis on a stylised rhythm or pattern in nature. The only device he retained from the pre-war paintings was the use of a lane or hedge to lead the viewer into the painting but it is now used without the usual accompanying fall in the fore-ground which gave the earlier paintings such a sense of vista and movement. *December Sunshine, Angus* (1949, pl. 30) is typical of many that followed it, with the lane and its wall turning into the picture, a stream alongside it and trees following the curve of the road. These trees, however, are not the formal stylisations of those in *Springtime in Eskdale* but are painted with an eye not just for shape but also for verisimilitude. *Borland Mill, Kirkmichael* (1950, pl. 32) and *The Knapp Mill, Rossie Priory* (1950, pl. 31) confirmed his new approach, with nature being celebrated by a naturalistic rendering of the view in front of the painter. These paintings are almost portraits of the landscape, painted with a sincere feeling for its inimitable qualities and evoking in the viewer something of the rapport with nature which the painter has developed over the years. Some of them really are portraits of trees, such as *The White Poplar* and *Bridge on the Knapp Road*. He believes he is almost mystic about trees and plant life, saying that he feels he should apologise to the grasses and plants that he damages as he sets up his easel in the corner of a field.

Watercolour became a much more important medium for him, too, graduating from the loose sketches which had formed the basis of the 1930s paintings into finished works in their own right. Following the show of his war-time sketches in 1946, The Fine Art Society exhibited a group of new watercolours of Scottish subjects in 1948 which was very successful and convinced him of the value of the medium. Like the oils, they are always painted outside and in recent years they have, perhaps, become his favoured medium. He has made his work in watercolour resemble a freely painted oil, strong in colour with enough detail to mark it as the work of McIntosh Patrick but stopping far short of the overworked definition of Birket Foster or W H Hunt. "Watercolour is much more fun", he says, and when the way that you paint involves setting up an easel in a corner of a field or on an unmade track in all weathers, sometimes warming up the paint before it will flow properly, the the immediacy and fluidity of watercolour must be a welcome change. The extra speed which the medium gives him allows his watercolours to be a much more accurate record of the weather at a specific moment, which in his oils is aways compromised by the time taken to finish a painting. He can work at a prodigious rate in watercolour but never so quickly nor with so much enthusiasm as he did in the first six months of 1973. In the autumn of 1972 he was taken suddenly and gravely ill and only an emergency operation saved his life. After several weeks of convalescence he was impatient to return to his painting and with a sense of relief and gratitude for his recovery he produced a fine series of forty watercolours which were shown at The Fine Art Society in Edinburgh in 1973.

In all of the paintings produced since 1950 Patrick has sought to show the rhythms and patterns which occur naturally in the landscape. He admits to being selective only of his viewpoint, choosing to point out to us the naturally occurring formations which he previously had had to invent.

As I got to know the countryside better and better, I came to realise that rhythmic ideas are inside you and so you go around looking for landscapes where the countryside fits a pre-conceived idea that you have inside you which you recognise when you see it. In other words, a twisted bit of wood, a wall or a gate, immediately causes you to say "Ah, that's the bit I'm looking for."

Now if you go back and look at my early pictures, which were made up in the studio, you'll find that they are the same only I didn't realise at that time that you could find what you wanted in nature. It DOES exist and you CAN find the same arrangements in the countryside and I don't have to invent them any more.

Realism, or naturalism, is much more difficult than what I was painting in the 1930s. It's much easier in lots of ways to make up a picture than to paint nature as it appears before us. Despite this, I still do it because I grew towards it and now I can't stop.

I think I'm just a realist, that's all . . . of a certain kind of subject. I don't suppose there's much sentimentality about my paintings but I have a deep feeling that Nature is immensely dignified when you're out of doors. I'm stuck by the dignity of everything. That's a human concept of course, nothing to do with trees themselves.

Since the war Patrick has probably got to know the trees, farms and lanes within twenty miles of Dundee better than any one else ever could. The titles of his paintings are a gazetteer of Angus farms and Perthshire hills, a litany which has been repeated with endless variation for forty years. Tullybaccart, Kingoodie, Abernyte, Lundie, Errol, Balshando, Birkhill, Carse of Gowrie, Longforgan, Dron — all have appeared on the walls of The Fine Art Society, the Royal Academy and the Royal Scottish Academy since the early 1950s. Patrick had retained his part-time lecturing post at the College of Art and in 1956 was appointed Visiting Artist at Hospitalfield House, the post-graduate study centre near Abroath. It was at this time that he painted a series of pictures of *Arbirlot Mill* (pls. 35–37), of which one of the mill lade shows how he was still prepared to experiment with different compositions and changes in handling. A more prolonged contact with young painters might have made him look with a different eye at his own work but a less expected surprise came from the Royal Academy. In 1956 his pictures were rejected, although they had been accepted since the war and continued to be hung from 1957 up to 1962, and the experience made Patrick take stock of his position. It coincided with a difference of opinion about his contract with Mr Grouse at The Fine Art Society and the combination of the two factors persuaded Patrick that he should pay more attention to exhibiting in Scotland than London. In 1949, he had been elected an Associate of the Royal Scottish Academy and a member of the Royal Institute of Oil Painters, but he was never to be elected to the Royal Academy in London. Before the war he had been runner-up in an election of Associates but ten years later the Council of the Academy had changed and Patrick's pre-war supporters were all dead, retired or outnumbered by a faction which was not in tune with his work. Throughout the 1950s and 1960s he consolidated his popular reputation throughout Scotland, becoming a full Academician in 1957, and at the same time achieving an international recognition through the publication of reproductions of many of his paintings. Patrick's paintings of Scotland have a place in many an expatriate home, replacing the image of a wild and dramatic landscape with a more douce and settled vision.

"It's not that I paint what I see, more that I see what I paint" is his description of his methods today. He is fond of telling the story of standing in front of his easel in a field and contemplating an almost finished painting when he was approached by a woman who looked at the picture, then looked across the field to the hills beyond, and then turned to him and said, "When will you put in the pylons?" Patrick looked up and saw them for the first time and replied, "Do you know, they hadn't even registered!" He creates his paintings before he puts brush to canvas by his selection of the view in front of him. He knows by long experience that by moving a foot or two to the left or right, backward or forward, he can change the whole emphasis of his composition. It is almost as if he first holds up an imaginary picture frame and collects within it the quintessence of a particular landscape. Indeed, he will pick up a cardboard window-mount in his studio and hold it against his paintings to show you that there are any number of individual subjects inside his pictures.

For forty years Patrick has held up this frame against the Angus landscape, in sun, wind, rain and snow. It is a rare combination of weather that will force him to seek the shelter of his car, to continue to paint while the rain streams down his window. It has encouraged in him not just new techniques of painting but ever more ingenious methods of keeping his canvas or paper dry, his paint fluid and his hands and feet warm. To follow such a solitary occupation one might think him a very private and retiring figure but the opposite is in fact the case. Whether his lonely life out in the Angus hills is the cause or the effect, back home in his house in Dundee he is gregarious and a prodigious talker. He has a seemingly endless supply of artistic stories, all wittily told, and is much in demand as a public speaker. He needs no preparation, "I just stand up and talk," he says, "and people seem to find it interesting." Whether the subject be his garden, his painting, the landscape or just himself (some say his favourite subject), he has a lot to say and all of it is delivered with the same enthusiasm and conviction that he conveys in his painting. In Dundee and Tayside he has become something of an institution, "Mainly because I'm now so old!", but the Honorary Degrees and other public awards conferred upon him are as much a mark of respect for the man as his work.

While he finds his popular acclaim pleasing, as he never wished to paint 'difficult' pictures and sees little point in painting squalor and misery, he will admit to a disappointment in the critics' lack of interest in his current work. He feels he has never courted popularity and that he has a valid statement to make in his work but that its immediate acceptance by the public has been held against him by post-war critics. 'Photographic' – the most frequent critical comment about his paintings – he finds particularly disconcerting as he believes that he is creating an illusion of reality through light and colour and not merely detailed brushwork.

People say I'm copying Nature. Well, I wish I could; wouldn't that be wonderful to be the equal of Nature; nobody can do that. People who think that about my work have never looked at Nature. No, it's just plain silly.

In fact, in many of his post-1960 works the detail has been softened to the point of suggestion rather than deliberation as his brush became more loaded with paint and a fine impasto took the place of the careful touch of his earlier paintings. It is the quality of his vision that creates the sense of reality, not his technique, and it is this that he feels is often misunderstood. His achievements in the 1930s have been undermined by the immediate popularity of his pictures, largely brought about by their early reproduction as collotypes by Harold Dickins, just as the more recent reproductions of his paintings have gained him another audience who may never have seen an original

Patrick. An often repeated critical comment of his work has been that the popular acceptance of it is due to its lack of intellectual input. From there, it has been an easy step to say that any painter who can be so popular can have nothing to say. Patrick's manual dexterity has been used in recent years to diminish his accomplishments but it is not just a recent phenomenon. Writing thirty years ago about McIntosh Patrick, Charles Carter, then Director of Aberdeen Art Gallery, identified the hurdles that the successful artist has to face:

There may be those who will look askance at such popularity; we are so accustomed to regarding the popular artist as a pot-boiler. Because many artistically worthless paintings have been popular we make the mistake of assuming that all popular paintings must be bad. The unrecognised of one generation have so often become the darlings of the next while the giants of the exhibition gallery have been as pygmies when transferred to the hall of fame, that we are reluctant to use the ready sale of an artist's work and his election to the academies as yardsticks by which to measure his achievement.
And we are right, artistic merit is not to be judged by such things. Disregarding them, it is always posterity which will award the laurels, laying them upon the tomb and not the brow of the artist; but his contemporaries cannot neglect such tangible evidence nor, because they must live, can artists. I recall hearing of two artists who were discussing the merits of their respective works in an exhibition. After one had referred to the abstract qualities and superior artistic merits of his own work, the other finally clinched the matter by saying, "Yes, but I've sold mine." It has not yet become an inevitable condemnation of a painting that it has found a buyer.

Patrick's work has always found buyers, and they were most welcome in the uncertain days of the 1930s. Most of his paintings sold in London and many were also exhibited across America and in the Empire. His popularity and success did not necessarily endear him to his Scottish colleagues, however, particularly since it was a success achieved in the south. His own position in Dundee, separate from the main artistic centres of Glasgow and Edinburgh, placed him in some isolation but it also enabled him to concentrate upon his chosen path without distraction. This was a two-edged sword, of course, in that it also meant that he was apart from the apparent mainstream of developments in modern painting in Scotland. But Patrick has remained faithful to his own beliefs and principles. He has not sought popularity at the expense of his art nor followed the trends, of which he is very much aware, that have won the approval of the critics if it meant being disloyal to his own standards. He is, above all, a professional who lives and is judged by his work. He is not immune to criticism; there have been times when he has questioned what he has done in the light of the comments of his peers but, ultimately, he has remained convinced that his work is valid in the terms of what he wishes to achieve and the means at his disposal. Posterity may award the artistic laurels upon his tomb but in doing so will only confirm the long-held conviction of the many admirers of his work, that he is one of the most accomplished painters of his generation who has won, through hard work and vision, a special place in the artistic hall of fame.

Roger Billcliffe

Plate 1 **Dorothea Hannah** 1928 Oil 20 × 26 The Artist's Family

Plate 2 **Les Baux** 1927 Oil 28 × 36 Private Collection

Plate 3 **The Rt Rev Monsignor Canon Turner** 1932 Oil 44 × 30 Dundee Art Galleries and Museums

Plate 4 **St Francis, Assisi** 1935 Oil 30 × 40 National Gallery of South Africa

Plate 5 **Glencoe** 1933-4 Oil 31 × 41 Texas Instruments Incorporated, Dallas

Plate 6 **Winter in Angus** 1935 Oil 30 × 40 Tate Gallery, London

Plate 7 **Marion** 1935 Oil 16 × 12 The Artist's Family

Plate 8 **Midsummer in East Fife** 1936 Oil 30 × 40 Aberdeen Art Gallery & Museums

Plate 9 **Sidlaw Village, Winter** 1936 Oil 28 × 36 Private Collection

Plate 10 **Autumn, Kinnordy** 1936 Oil 30 × 40 Dundee Art Galleries & Museums

Plate 11 **The Ettrick Shepherd** 1937 Oil 30 × 40 Manchester City Art Galleries

Plate 12 **An Exmoor Farm** 1938 Oil 34 × 51 Ferens Art Gallery, Hull City Museums & Art Galleries

Plate 13 **Springtime in Eskdale** 1938 Oil 30 × 40 National Museums & Art Galleries on Merseyside (Walker Art Gallery)

Plate 14 **Winter in Perthshire** 1938 Oil 30 × 40 Private Collection

Plate 15 **Traquair House** 1938 Oil 13 × 17½ Private Collection

Plate 16 **Stobo Kirk** 1936 Oil 20 × 24 City of Edinburgh Museums & Art Galleries

Plate 17b **Poster for Harrow Weald, London Transport:
Longer Days are Here Again** 1938 The Artist's Family

Plate 17a **Poster for Harrow Weald, London Transport:
Happy Days of Cheer Again** 1938 The Artist's Family

Plate 18 **A City Garden** 1940 Oil 28 × 36 Dundee Art Galleries & Museums

Plate 19 **Captain The Lord Lyell VC** 1940 Oil 36 × 28 The Lady Lyell

Plate 20 **Sidi bin Said from la Marsa, Tunisia** 1943
Pen & ink & watercolour 9 × 12 The Artist's Family

Plate 22 **Volturno at Capua** 1945
Watercolour 12 × 18 The Artist's Family

Plate 21 **Villas on the Mediterranean, Tunisia** 1943
Watercolour 5 × 7 The Artist's Family

Plate 23 **Trefilisco Caserta** 1945
Watercolour 12½ × 15½ Dundee Art Galleries & Museums

Plate 24 **Glamis Village** 1940 Oil 28 × 36 National Museums & Art Galleries on Merseyside (Lady Lever Art Gallery)

Plate 25 **Glamis Village in April** 1946 Oil 18 × 24 Robert Fleming Holdings Limited

53

Plate 26 **Arlie Castle** 1946 Oil 20 × 27 The Earl of Arlie

Plate 27 **Dryburgh Abbey – Design for a Railway Poster** c.1947 Oil on board 30 × 48 Mrs Velendia White

Plate 28 **Unthank Farm** 1947 Oil 28 × 36 Viscount Leverhulme

Plate 29 **Tay Bridge from my Studio Window** 1948 Oil 30 × 40 Dundee Art Galleries & Museums

Plate 30 **December Sunshine, Angus** 1949 Oil 30 × 40 Private Collection

Plate 31 **Knapp Mill, Rossie Priory** 1950 Oil 30 × 40 Private Collection

Plate 32 **Boreland Mill, Kirkmichael** 1950 Oil 28 × 36 Perth Museum & Art Gallery

Plate 33 **The Edge of the Quarry, Loch Eil – Nature Imitating Art** c.1952 Watercolour 11½ × 15 Private Collection

Plate 34 **The Bridge, Den o'Fowlis, Angus** 1957 Oil 25 × 30 Glasgow Art Gallery & Museum

Plate 35 **Cornstacks near Lundie** 1957 Oil 20 × 24 James King

Plate 36 **Glamis Castle** 1960 Oil 28 × 36 HRH The Princess Margaret, Countess of Snowdon

Plate 37 **The Mill Lade, Arbirlot** 1958 Oil 24 × 30 Mrs D R McIntyre, Dundee

Plate 38 **Kinfauns,** 1964 Oil 28 × 36 Mr & Mrs C P Hammett

Plate 39 **The Lane, Milnfield** 1962 Oil 30 × 40 Perth Museum & Art Gallery

Plate 40 **The Crags of Lundie** 1964 Oil 30 × 40 Richard Green

Plate 41 **Sidlaw Vista from Muirhead** 1964 Oil 28 × 36 Murray Burns

Plate 42 **The Tay Road Bridge** 1966 Oil 25 × 30 Dundee Art Galleries & Museums

Plate 43 **Berry-picking, Mains of Gray** 1967 Oil 25 × 30 Private Collection

Plate 44 **The Drinking Pool, Benvie** 1967 Oil 20 × 24 Mr & Mrs L S Fraser

Plate 45 **The Old Sawmill and Forester's House, Rossie Priory** 1974 Watercolour 21 × 29 Private Collection

Plate 46 **Ancient Trees, Mains of Gray, Invergowrie** 1970 Oil 28 × 36 Private Collection

Plate 47 **Pitcur Den, Autumn** 1969 Oil 25 × 30 Private Collection

Plate 48 **Avenue, Springtime** 1971 Oil 25 × 30 Private Collection

Plate 49 **Thriepley, near Lundie, Angus** 1971 Oil 30 × 40 Mr & Mrs Sandy Saddler

Plate 50 **Murroes Bridge** 1976 Oil 25 × 30 Royal Scottish Academy

Plate 51 **Cleish Mill, near Thriepley** 1982 Oil 36 × 48 The Artist's Family

Plate 52 **Dundee from Dron** 1972 Watercolour 22 × 29½ Private Collection

Plate 53 **Near Luthrie, Fife** 1979 Oil 28 × 36 Grampian Television

Plate 54 **A City Garden** 1979 Acrylic 30 × 44 Dundee Art Galleries & Museums

Plate 55 **The Artist's Studio** 1984 Watercolour 21 × 29 Macfarlane Group (Clansman) PLC

Plate 56 **My Garden under Snow** 1979 Watercolour 28 × 20 Private Collection

Plate 57 **The Tay Bridge in Winter** 1980 Watercolour 20 × 28 Private Collection

Plate 58 **The Field Gate, Keithick** 1981 Watercolour 29 × 21 Mr & Mrs John Hart

Plate 59 **Balshando Farm** 1985 Oil 36 × 48 Macfarlane Group (Clansman) PLC

CATALOGUE

Unless otherwise stated, all works in oil are on canvas and all works in pencil or watercolour are on paper. Sizes are in inches, height before width.

1 Near Ghent 1922 *(fig. 1)*
Watercolour 13 × 9½
The Artist's Family

2 Keithick Mill 1923 *(frontispiece)*
Oil 14 × 18
The Artist's Family

**3 Wellington Church from Park
Circus, Glasgow** 1925 *(fig. 7)*
Pencil & watercolour 6 × 7½
The Artist's Family

4 Trinity College, Glasgow 1925
(fig. 8)
Pencil 9 × 6
The Artist's Family

**5 The Forth & Clyde Canal, Port
Dundas, Glasgow** 1925 *(fig. 9)*
Pencil & watercolour 8 × 6½
The Artist's Family

**6 The Portico, Glasgow Art
Gallery** 1925
(fig. 10)
Pencil & watercolour 7½ × 6½
The Artist's Family

**7 The Forth & Clyde Canal,
Dawsholm, Glasgow** 1925
(fig. 11)
Pencil & watercolour 5 × 7
The Artist's Family

**8 Farm at Balmuildy, near
Glasgow** 1925
(fig. 12)
Pencil & watercolour 7 × 8
The Artist's Family

9 Avignon 1926 *(fig. 13)*
Pen & Ink & watercolour 7 × 9½
The Artist's Family

10 Bruges 1926
Etching 6 × 6
The Artist's Family

11 The Ramparts, Carcassonne
1927
Etching 7½ × 6
The Artist's Family

12 A Quaint Corner of Avignon
1927
Etching 8½ × 6
The Artist's Family

13 Carcassonne – la Cité 1927
Etching 6 × 8
The Artist's Family

14 Street Scene, Provence 1927
Etching 6 × 8½
The Artist's Family

15 Provençal Church 1927
Etching 6 × 7
The Artist's Family

16 Evening, Nîmes 1927 *(fig. 4)*
Etching 6 × 7½
The Artist's Family

**17 Course des Taureaux aux
Arènes – Arles** 1927
Etching 6 × 4
The Artist's Family

18 Tarascon 1927
Etching 6 × 8½
The Artist's Family

19 The Egotist 1927 *(fig. 2)*
Oil 39 × 63
The Artist's Family

20 Study for *The Egotist* 1927
Watercolour 13 × 21
The Artist's Family

21 Les Ramparts, Les Baux 1927
(fig. 3)
Etching 7 × 10
The Artist's Family

22 Les Baux 1927 *(pl. 2)*
Oil 28 × 36
Private Collection

23 Les Baux, Provence 1928
Etching 7 × 10
The Artist's Family

24 Palais des Papes, Avignon
1928 *(fig. 5)*
Etching 5 × 8½
The Artist's Family

25 Dorothea Hannah 1928 *(pl. 1)*
Oil 20 × 26
The Artist's Family

26 The Three Sisters Glencoe
1928
Etching 7 × 10
The Artist's Family

**27 The Pass of Glencoe from the
Valley** 1928 *(fig. 6)*
Etching 6 × 8
The Artist's Family

28 Loch Lomond 1928
Etching 5 × 8½
The Artist's Family

29 The Pillars, Dundee 1928
Watercolour 9 × 12
Lent by Dundee Art Galleries &
Museums

**30 Strathmartine's Lodgings, the
Vault, Dundee** 1928
Watercolour 9 × 11½
Lent by Dundee Art Galleries &
Museums

**31 Interior of the Yarn Store, Old
Glamis Factory** 1929
Oil 18 × 14
Lent by the Misses Donald

32 Wade's Bridge, Garve 1929
Etching 4½ × 10
The Artist's Family

33 Ben Slioch, Loch Maree 1929
Oil 30 × 40
Private Collection

34 Ben Slioch, Loch Maree c.1930
Etching, unpublished – 3 states
7 × 10
The Artist's Family

35 Assisi 1930 *(fig. 14)*
Oil 12 × 16
The Artist's Family

36 Alexander Russell 1931
Oil 24 × 20
Lent by Duncan of Jordanstone
College of Art, Dundee

**37 The Rt Rev Monsignor Canon
Turner** 1932
(pl. 3)
Oil 44 × 30
Lent by Dundee Art Galleries &
Museums

38 Glencoe c.1932/3
Pen & ink & watercolour
10 × 14
The Artist's Family

39 Glencoe 1933–4
(pl. 5)
Oil 31 × 41
Lent by Texas Instruments
Incorporated, Dallas

40 Loch Etive 1933
Etching 6 × 8½
The Artist's Family

41 Wade's Bridge 1934
Oil 18 × 21
Private Collection

42 Evening in the Border Country
c.1934
Watercolour 11 × 22
Lent by The Fine Art Society

43 Assisi c.1934
Etching 5½ × 8
The Artist's Family

44 Stobo Kirk c.1934
Etching 4 × 6
The Artist's Family

45 Rocky landscape, Ross-shire
c.1935
Etching 6 × 8
The Artist's Family

46 Winter in Angus 1935
(pl. 6)
Oil 30 × 40
Lent by the Trustees of the Tate
Gallery